The Ultimate Guide to Making Your Husband Happy

Mary Jensen

TABLE OF CONTENTS

25 Intimate Ways to Please Your Husband

Marriage is a beautiful journey that brings happiness, peace, and contentment to the couple, but it also demands effort from both partners to maintain a healthy union. If you're looking for tips on making your spouse smile, read on as we provide some romantic and efficient ways to make your spouse smile.

All a husband really wants from his wife is her sincere love, care, and concern; he doesn't expect pricey gifts and treats at 5-star hotels. Continue reading as we share some intriguing suggestions for ways to win over your husband and win his love. Every relationship experiences difficult times, but what keeps the connection strong is the love and willingness to work through them. But keep in mind that you shouldn't push yourself to do something just to win his favor. You ought to be willingly carrying out this action out of pure love for your husband.

1. Perform his favorite actions

Doing your husband's favorite things for him is one way to keep him pleased. You might prepare his favorite dessert, meet him for lunch at his preferred restaurant, or make his favorite cup of coffee. You can converse with him about his interests or simply sit together and watch his preferred programs.

2. I loved him deeply

After picking him up from work, take him to his preferred outdoor location with a picnic lunch. Make a list of the locations he wants to go on romantic dates. It might be in front of a fire, on the sand, under water, on a rooftop, or in the light of the moon. Sometimes, these actions can make him feel cherished and content.

3. Shower together

When was the last time you and your husband

both took a shower? By asking your husband to the shower with you, you can spend some quiet time together. These simple gestures will make your husband smile. It's possible to connect deeply through intimacy, which need not always be sexual.

4. Make minimal concessions

Doing a few things that your spouse enjoys is one of the best ways to keep him pleased. Participate in activities that your husband enjoys if you want to make him happy. You can join him for a workout or a run.

5. Maintain your attractiveness

You are better able to care for those you love when you put your needs first. Without any sense of vanity, you want to give it everything you've got not out of any sense of vanity. So, improve your fitness and dress beautifully to wow your partner.

6. Make arrangements to go to his hometown

Bring your husband back to his more enjoyable moments. Think about your husband's reaction if you plan a trip down memory lane for him. Visit his former school, stroll by his old house, and go to the playground where he used to play. You will grow closer to your hubby as a result. If you can't physically go, ask him about some of his favorite childhood memories.

7. Set up a gathering with your pals

Plan a get-together for his closest pals. It can involve a quick trip and a dinner date with his pals and their partners. It might take more time and effort, but it will brighten your husband's day.

8. Make your feelings known

If you want your husband to be pleased, don't be afraid to use those sweet, romantic gestures. Try slipping love letters into his wallet or lunchbox. These actions will make your husband feel pampered once more.

9. Respect him

Recognize his efforts in maintaining the family's unity and improving your life on a daily basis. Reiterate your love for him and express how valuable he is to you. Praise him and express your pride in him if he wins a mini-marathon or receives a promotion. He will experience joy and confidence as a result.

10.   Be upbeat

If you want your husband to be content, having a heart will be useful. If you are unhappy, miserable, and irritable all the time in life, he won't be get rid of negative feelings like anger and dissatisfaction if you want your husband to be happy. Instead, saturate your heart with thanksgiving, optimism, and joy.

11.   Make his experience valuable

Before making any significant decisions, get your husband's perspective and let him know you appreciate and respect his viewpoints. This will give him a sense of importance in the marriage. It will instill in him a sense of obligation and accountability in daily life.

12.   Delay in assigning blame

Your husband might blunder or act carelessly, or he might forget to do something. Don't be rough on him when this occurs; be tolerant. Make him aware of his error and gently warn him not to make the same mistake again.

13.   Don't be a nag.

Every husband's biggest nightmare is a nagging wife. You are misguided if you think that bugging your husband would make him a better person. Never ignore or minimize your husband if you want to make him happy. You don't have to tolerate all of his errors, though. You can gently point them out to him to get him to stop doing them.

14.   Recognize him

Respect your husband the way he deserves to be treated. Never try to influence your husband's decisions; rather, respect his ideas and beliefs. After all, he respects and admires you in the same ways, and that is what makes for a good marriage.

15.   Do not attempt to alter him

Making comparisons between your partner and other men will only infuriate and annoy him. He will consequently become resentful and distant. You will drive your husband away from you if you try to shape him into the person you want him to be. Even if he never finds out, doing this will alter how you feel about him and how you come across to him.

16.   Let him be who he is

Love your husband and accept him as he is allow him to express himself and speak his thoughts, and emphasize his wise decisions while downplaying his errors. Never criticize him excessively and always take the time to acknowledge his good deeds.

17.   Get rid of the little things

Keep your mind off of small irritations if you want your husband to be happy. Many unions end in divorce for trivial reasons. Avoid exaggerating little concerns and turning them into major problems. Put it behind you and concentrate on the positive aspects.

18.   Give him gifts

Whether you go on a trip or simply go shopping, buy him a gift. Let him know that you value and think about him. You are not required to give him pricey presents. Any item he would adore having, such as a shirt or a bottle of perfume, will make him pleased.

19.   Love more frequently

Spending time on enhancing your sexual activities is one way to make your marriage more joyful. Marriage might get boring at times. So make time for him and liven up your sexual life. One of the few special experiences you can only have with your partner is making love.

20.   Hug him

Your husband will remain content if you give him a regular dose of passionate kissing, snuggling, or hugging. Therefore, kiss him frequently, just as you did when you first started dating.

21.   Make him your closest pal

Invest in your friendship if you want your husband to be happy. Spend time doing the things that you and your partner like to do together. As you would with friends, have fun, work hard, play, and converse.

22.   Practicing romanticism

Avoid being stuck in a mundane routine with your spouse. Mix in a touch of romanticism and whimsy. Try simple romantic gestures like scheduling a candlelit dinner or going for a stroll in the park if you want to make your husband happy

23.   Give him room

Give your husband the room he needs to enjoy his hobbies. Give him time to work on himself and exhort him to pursue his passions.

24.   Embrace him with a warm smile

Who wouldn't want to return home every evening to a friendly smile? When a smile can set the tone for the rest of the day, what better time is there to tell your husband you love him than first thing in the morning? Put your fatigue or other thoughts aside for a while so you can make his day better with your warm, caring smile.

25.   Demonstrate enthusiasm for his interests

One approach to making your husband happy is to find out about his interests and hobbies. Finding out about your husband's interests demonstrates your concern for him and helps you get to know him better. While you don't have to have the same interests as your husband to enjoy his joy, it's still crucial to show interest in him.

There are various ways you can make your partner happy. Some of these can be done with very little effort; they are just basic movements. Your life will be happier too, and you can have a happy marriage if you can figure out how to make your husband happy and he reciprocates.

You have 15 ways to win your husband over and increase his love for you.

It is not difficult to wow your man and win his heart, and if you put your best effort forward, you will be able to achieve this goal with ease. Here are some tips on how to make sure that throughout the day, your husband thinks of you first:

1. Showcase Your Feelings

Men can experience insecurity because they cannot read minds. Your partner might believe that he isn't making you happy if you don't show him that you love him. So, establish the practice of expressing your affection for him by telling him how much he means to you or by doing small acts of kindness for him. Put a message saying "I love you" on the bathroom mirror, or put some love notes in his wallet or pockets. He'll be startled to find it, and he'll be grinning when he does. These modest displays of affection will also show him that you keep him in your thoughts even when he is not present.

2. Prepare some food for him

Take this advice: "The route to a man's heart is through his stomach." Prepare a special meal for your loving husband to impress him. Prepare his favorite meal and watch him savor it. Whatever you prepare, he will adore it, but the work you put into it will mean more to him. You have nothing to worry about if you can cook well. To show him how much his pleasure matters to you, bake him his favorite cake or prepare his favorite dish.

3. Discover his interests

Even if you don't have a passion for either sports or cars, trying to understand your husband's interests is usually beneficial. He might want to go on road trips, go hiking, or watch movies. You might find that the two of you end up having a fantastic time together, bonding over something that means so much to him if you ask him to tell you about his interests and demonstrate how things function.

4. Think about a surprise weekend getaway.

Consider exploring new sexual possibilities if you want to know how to make your partner feel special Sometimes all your relationship needs to rekindle the romance is a change of location. If you can, arrange a trip to a place that both you and your partner would find romantic. Make reservations for a hotel or homestay and plan a surprise visit for your hubby. Your hubby would be appreciative of the pleasant surprise and the change of scenery.

5. Make Out with Him

Do you recall the times when the two of you first started dating, when your days and nights were dominated by calls and nonstop texting? There must have been so much excitement that you two might not have been able to control your flirting. You might not have time to flirt or text frequently right now. Consider going back to those times. One tiny way to reclaim the humor and affection that used to come so readily to you when you were with your husband is to flirt with him. You can give him a kiss while no one is looking or send him flirtatious texts.

6. Together, they watch a romantic film

If your husband had a demanding day at work and needs to unwind, watching a movie together is a terrific idea. Have dinner with him when he gets home, and then you can both watch a movie of his choosing. Hold his hand while you both watch the movie. It is possible to have a romantic evening at home with dinner and a movie. In truth, it can also be much more private.

7. Schedule a date night

Nothing is more desired by a married couple, especially when children are present, than some time alone. Make sure you arrange for someone to watch your children while you organize a date night with your partner. You should make this effort since you two should always have time to get to know one another and reinvigorate the passion in your relationship.

8. Communicate

Communication is the key to keeping any connection strong over time. Talk to your partner; be open and sincere. Be honest with him about your feelings. If you both find it difficult to make time for one another, discuss it. Talk about how to schedule time for each. There will always be other factors that could enter into your relationship, but it is your responsibility to ensure that they never harm it. Make time for your partner and communicate with him. You'll both realize how much you love each other when you have an honest chat.

9. Establish a Love Nest

By surprising your husband with a romantic atmosphere in your bedroom at night, you can increase your intimacy with him. Bring a bottle of wine and use candles to decorate your room. To get the mood right, try serving chocolate-dipped strawberries. Put some rose petals on your bed and light some scented candles in your room. Your hubby will undoubtedly appreciate your efforts. And because you went to the trouble to make a private, intimate setting for the two of you to express your love, he will want you even more.

10.   Gifts for Him as a Surprise

Men can also become really delighted by presents; it's not just ladies who enjoy receiving them. Even modest and thoughtful gifts will do the trick; there is no need to go all out. For instance, if your spouse enjoys playing video games, getting him a new game CD will please him

How to Make Your Husband like You Individually

Sometimes you need to make an impression on your husband by being the person that you are; it's not always about the romantic things you do for him. Here are some ways to make an impression on him personally:

11.   Treat yourself

There's a cliché that goes, "happy wife, happy life," and it's not entirely untrue. A woman who is overworked and stressed out may get agitated and distracted, making it difficult for her to take care of herself and her home. A woman needs to take time for herself every now and then to go to the spa, get a much-needed massage, or even just get a facial at the salon because of all the things she has to juggle in her life. You can take charge of your life, impress your partner, and control your life when you're calm and stress-free.

12.   Maintaining Your Health

Keep yourself and your family healthy for the sake of your husband, children, and family.

You will be able to care for your husband more effectively if you eat healthy foods and have a healthy lifestyle. You won't be able to care for your husband at all if you are prone to illnesses as a result of poor self-care. To keep your body and mind healthy, eat a nutritious, balanced diet and exercise frequently.

13.   Acquire Knowledge

Your expertise might also make an impression on your partner. Men adore women who can hold a deep conversation and are knowledgeable about a variety of topics. He will be happy with you if you attend an event with him and are able to strike up a conversation with his buddies about various topics. You are sure to be a success at all the dinner parties you go to with him, from his parents to his coworkers. Make it a practice to read the most recent news each day, and if you haven't already, start reading books.

14.   He became his close friend

You play a significant role because you are your husband's closest friend in life. You will know how to treat your husband by realizing that you are not just his wife, but also his closest friend. Have fun with him; joke around, laugh, do stupid things, and be there for him in quiet if that's what he needs. Also, give him support when he needs it and praise him when he does something right. Your husband will need and want you more if you are the only person he can be completely himself with.

15.   Honor His "Alone Time"

Your man needs his time with his buddies or even by himself, just as you need your time with your girlfriends. . Spending time with the boys can give a man a new life and make him feel young again, even if you might be the center of his universe. Even though you might not enjoy it, he needs it, and he will love and respect you even more for being patient enough to give him his space.

A man and wife's relationship must be healthy because marriage is a significant component of a person's life. People don't just live happily ever after like in fairy tales and movies; it takes work. Being the wife who loves and supports her husband in all aspects of his life, whether at home, in the bedroom, or outdoors, is your duty in order to contribute to his happiness.

21

How to Get Your Husband to Respect You in 20 Healthy Ways

Maybe you should consider looking at how you treat your husband if you want him to respect you more. Do you revere him sufficiently? Do you treat him the way a wife would treat a husband? Respect breeds respect, as the saying goes. Why not first work on how you treat your husband with respect in order to earn his respect?

See how you can earn your husband's respect by following these guideline

1. Don't cut him off when he's talking.

Allowing your husband to speak without

interjecting is one way to respect him. Your husband experiences the same irritation you do anytime someone speaks over you while you are conversing. Therefore, wait for him to finish speaking before responding.

1. Listen to him anytime he speaks to you.

Your husband will feel valued if you offer him your undivided attention every time you speak, in addition to refraining from interacting with him while you speak. So, while you are having a discussion, keep your phone, switch off the TV, or turn away from the computer.

2. Stay away from harsh criticism of him.

Because he is only human, your partner undoubtedly has flaws. But whenever you are disappointed in him, talk to him calmly rather than scold him in front of him. Point out his errors without becoming offensive. Try to calmly express your worry to him, explaining the consequences of his poor decisions and offering some suggestions for how he might behave better.

3. Don't evaluate him against others.

Being compared to others is not only hurtful but also disrespectful. So don't make comparisons between your hubby and other men. You must acknowledge that he is unique among them and that he possesses particular advantages.

4. Discuss him favorably in front of your children.

The upbringing of your kids to be moral people is your duty as a parent. Respect for others, especially their parents, is a quality you should foster in them. Teach kids to respect their father regardless of his flaws. Praise him in front of the kids to start doing this.

5. In front of others, give him praise.

By encouraging your husband around other people, you can show your admiration for him in yet another way. Do not humiliate him in front of others by exposing his negative characteristics. Instead, praise him in front of them.

6. Never yell at him.

Every time he yells at you, you don't feel respected, do you? And he shares the same sentiment. Because of this, refrain from yelling at him, even if you are furious with him and especially if others are present.

7. Do not bug him.

Generally speaking, wives are niggles. Although not all wives are like this, many husbands lament having nagging partners. Stop being a nag if you want your husband to respect you.

8. Stay away from disagreeing with him in front of the kids.

It's common for husbands and wives to have misunderstandings. Fighting in front of your kids, however, is not a good idea. In addition to having a negative effect on your children, feeling guilty will make it more difficult for you and your husband to appreciate one another.

10. Quit complaining about him to your pals.

Your other half is your hubby. That is to say, if you continue to disparage him to others, you are also dissing yourself. Also, your husband will be very upset if he finds out, which will make it hard for you to earn his respect.

11. He is careful with his possessions.

You must treat your husband's possessions with the same respect if you want him to value yours. Take care not to damage, break, lose, or stain any of his possessions.

12. Allow him room in the house.

Your husband wants it too, much as you require private space at home. Therefore, let him set up his workspace or office within the home. He'll be grateful to you for sure.

13. Let him have the last say on everything.

According to the Bible, husbands are supposed to be the family's head. Indicating that they ought to be in charge. However, it does not imply that you are a lesser member of the family. On the contrary, you are both on the same level. You just have different roles, and one of your roles is to make sure the family's decisions are final.

14. Never challenge him in front of people, especially your kids.

It's necessary to appear strong in front of the kids and other people, in addition to not fighting with your husband in their presence. Never voice your disagreement in front of others. He will feel embarrassed if you contradict him in front of others. He can also lose other people's respect.

15. He meets his requirements in bed.

As a wife, it is your job to fulfill your husband's sexual needs, and the same goes for him. Therefore, unless there is a valid excuse, such as the fact that you are ill, do not decline his requests for physical intimacy at any time they are made.

16. Ensure your own wellbeing.

Never take yourself for granted, no matter how busy you are taking care of your family. Instead, treat yourself the way you would if you were still single. Even though you are a busy mother and wife, taking care of your looks will help your husband respect you. It's because you can demonstrate to him you might and strength.

17. be respectful to his siblings and

parents.

If your husband realizes how much you value his family, he will definitely respect you. Even though they may not be ideal, your partner values your in-laws. You should therefore treat them nicely just for that reason.

18. Take his advice to heart.

If you ask your husband's opinion anytime you are having an issue, he will feel valued. Additionally, if he learns that his advice benefits you, he will be proud of himself. He would want to repay the favor by paying attention to you the next time as a result.

19. Before making any plans, talk to him.

You should involve your husband in your personal decisions if you want him to think about you before making them. Before making a decision, be open with him about your goals. He'll be urged to follow suit.

20. Ensure that he takes the family's spiritual direction.

Your husband is supposed to be the head of

the family, as was already mentioned. Encourage him to lead you and the kids in prayer and Bible sharing to help him rise to the role of being a spiritual leader. Your husband will be appreciative of you knowing that you are there for him.

15 Incredible Ways to Honor Your Husband and Strengthen Your Marriage

Simply treat your husband in the same manner that you want to be treated.

Mutual respect is what a relationship demands. Even if one partner fails in this area, it's possible that the other partner's relationship will suffer. If you're a woman wondering how to respect your spouse, you've come to the correct place. First though, what exactly is respect? There is more going on than just romance and pleasantries. It has a lot to do with how equally you treat your partner and how accepting you are of who they really are. Unfortunately, after a few years of marriage, people have a tendency to lose sight of this essential principle of respect for one another, which frequently leads to toxic relationships. An in-depth discussion of the reasons why you should respect your man as well as the top 15 strategies to do so will be provided in this post. So let's get going.

Why Is Your Husband Deserving of Respect?

Respect is a strong word with many different meanings. Respect can be seen in the context of a good relationship as a positive attitude and gratifying emotion for your partner. You can show your husband how much you appreciate him in many ways, such as with words, hugs, kisses, and other loving actions. Additionally, both parties take into account one another's demands. You show your husband respect by being aware of his wants and feelings, in addition to honoring the bond you two share.

When two people don't respect each other, they usually end up being very unhappy and angry. Will you believe it if your partner approaches you one day and declares, "I love you, but I do not respect you?" Do you believe that someone may love you while not honoring you? Respect and love go hand in hand. Because of this, love and respect are important parts of any relationship, including marriage.

But when it comes to showing respect, we frequently assume it stems from a position of weakness. It conjures up pictures of kids getting up to meet their teachers, workers being polite to their superiors, etc. However, respect in a marriage is very different. You are mistaken if you perceive it as inferior. If a wife respects her husband, it is not because she thinks she is less than him but rather because she cherishes and values their union. In a similar vein, a husband must respect his wife out of love for her.

You are in the perfect place if you want to show your husband more respect. Here are some ways to show your husband respect and build a relationship based on respect and admiration for each other.

1. **Give up seeking perfection**.

Despite being overused, the adage "nobody is flawless" is nonetheless accurate. Every human being works to the best of their abilities despite having a variety of skills. So be patient with your husband and accept him for who he is. Be analytical and critical of him and his choices, but not to an excessive degree. Only when you let go of the notion of a flawless marriage and a perfect husband will you be able to respect and accept your husband as he truly is.

2. Be Grateful for His Decisions

Building a family and getting married both take a lot of work. You may both need to work nonstop to find the ideal balance between work and family as a couple with children. Your husband must have made similar sacrifices for your family as you did. Therefore, respect his choices and his ability to properly fulfill the duty of supporting a family. Keep telling him how appreciative you are of him and his desire to take care of the family.

3. Once in a while, express gratitude.

Once the routine of a marriage takes hold, couples frequently forget to express gratitude to one another. Even when they are grateful, they do not freely show it and begin to take each other for granted. Avoid falling for this trap. Simply feeling grateful is insufficient; tell him so. Anytime you can, give your husband a hug. These two short phrases can have a significant impact on your husband and your marriage. To express your gratitude, you might also get him gifts, arrange a surprise date, or take him away for the weekend.

4. Be sure to Communicate Effectively

A successful marriage depends on effective communication. Make sure you are open with your husband if you desire his respect. Do not be afraid to bring up challenging topics even if you feel uncomfortable doing so. Keeping them inside will only cause you and your marriage more problems. Texting is one strategy for launching tough talks. Text him about it first if you're hesitant to talk to him in person about certain topics. When you feel a little more at ease, you can move on to having a face-to-face conversation.

5. Never contrast him with other men.

Nobody enjoys continually being told what they should and shouldn't do. It is detrimental to both you and your husband to constantly criticize him. Instead of comparing him to other men, focus on how ideal he is for you. You won't be content with him until you accept him for who he is.

6. Accept his family as though they were your own.

A marriage brings together not only the husband and wife, but also two families. You should treat his family with love and respect if you want him to join your family. One additional benefit is that you can always ask his family about his upbringing, his likes and dislikes, amusing anecdotes about him, etc. After that, you might include these memories in the presents you have in mind for him for his birthday and anniversaries.

7. Never criticize your husband in front of your children.

Young children's minds are impressionable. Talk politely about their father in front of the kids to help them grow up with a loving, affectionate, and respectful attitude toward him. Pay attention to his skills, personality quirks, and other things that make him a wonderful father and person. In addition, the children will benefit greatly from their father's personality, which will help them develop into well-rounded people.

8. Apologize if necessary.

You are not flawless, just as your husband is not. Making mistakes that can harm both you and your marriage is completely acceptable. In this scenario, do not shy away from apologizing to your husband and do not bring your ego into the scene. Apologizing when needed will guarantee healthy communication between you and your husband. Many significant problems in your relationship can be resolved with a sincere apology.

9. Be his personal cheerleader.

Even when their team is losing, the cheerleaders continue to support them. You must support your husband in the same way, no matter what his achievements or setbacks may be. This will give him the drive to work hard and the fortitude to get through challenging circumstances.

10.   Try Something New in Bed.

Physical and sexual intimacy are equally as important to marriage as emotional connection. A fulfilling sexual life will keep the fire burning in your marriage. Try new things in bed occasionally to keep your husband engaged. Additionally, the fact that you are prepared to do new things with him will demonstrate to him your love and respect for him. Be cautious, however, to only engage in consenting sexual activity with your husband

11.   Pray for him

If you have faith in God, please pray for your husband's health. Many Bible verses speak of respecting your husband, if you consider yourself to be a practicing Christian. But all religions promote respect for your spouse. Ask God to keep him safe from harm and grant him the courage and ability to deal with challenges. Not only will this benefit your husband, but it will also help you grow closer to God.

12.   Celebrate His Success

Your partner might also desire to spice up your sexual life, so you are not the only one who would like to do so. Be mindful of his emotional and physical advances. He may feel unwelcome and unwelcomed if his physical advances are ignored. At any time, politely let him know if you're not feeling sexual. However, cherish the physical as well as the emotional facets of your union.

13.   Give him some room.

Talking to your husband politely and giving him space are both important signs that you respect him. You do not necessarily have to spend every minute of every day together just because you share a life. Give him room to socialize with his friends and engage in his own interests. Similarly, you ought to have acquaintances and a separate existence from your spouse.

14.   Please pay attention to him.

There are many obligations that come with married life, such as raising children, taking care of the home and extended family, etc. You face a very real chance of running out of time and hurriedly completing tasks. Give your husband your complete attention when he is speaking, though. While you are listening to him, it can be alluring to complete a chore or two, but resist the urge. Maintain eye contact, pay close attention to what he says, and when he asks for it, give him suggestions and advise. This will demonstrate to him your regard for him and your concern for all of his Opinions.

15.　　　Alter Your Behavior And Attitude

You must alter your mindset in addition to your actions if you want to show your husband that you appreciate him. Even though it could be difficult to grasp how to respect your husband at first, once you begin going, it will grow easier and easier. All of your new attitudes and behaviors will soon become second nature, allowing you to easily achieve your objectives.

The basic truth is that for a relationship to succeed, respect is a two-way street that must run smoothly. You must ensure that your spouse respects you as we examine how to respect your husband. To create a healthy environment around you, support and appreciate one another. Sometimes you could respond in a way that makes your partner feel disrespectful. So, ensure that they feel safe telling you so that you may acknowledge your error and attempt to make it right. If there is a lot of respect in your relationship

, your love for one another will only expand.

11 suggestions for rekindling your husband's love for you

You want to know what you can do because you believe that your husband is losing interest in you.

Look, everyone experiences challenging times in their relationships. There will inevitably be moments when your husband seems to be falling in love with you and your marriage feels stale. The positive news

There are many things you may do to rekindle the flame and make things right.

Believe me, many married ladies have faced a similar predicament and have been able to successfully change the course of love.

Knowing more about male psychology and what makes men tick can make it much easier for you to make your husband fall in love with you all over again.

1. He should miss you.

I'm aware that this sounds a little odd. You know, genuinely spend time with him if you want to make your husband fall in love with you again. But bear with me.

For couples, sometimes time apart is beneficial. It offers you time to live your life on your own terms and develop personally.

You run the risk of developing co-dependency and a toxic relationship if you spend every waking hour together. That is NOT what you want, I assure you.

When your husband and you both get overly preoccupied with other pursuits, you both have much to talk about when you do get to spend time together.

The reality is as follows:

It's possible to create balance in your relationship by taking time apart.

What's more, and most crucially, it offers you an opportunity to miss each other.

Most people discover their love for someone when they are not present.

He'll notice how much he misses you after some time apart from you, and if he does, it will undoubtedly rekindle the fire in his belly.

I discovered this and many more from renowned relationship guru Bradley Browning As far as keeping marriages together goes, Brad is the real deal. Millions of copies of his books have been sold, and he offers wise counsel on his well-liked YouTube channel.

Here is a great free video where he talks about how he fixes marriages in a unique way.

2. Respect yourself.

Sounds silly? Sure. But how can you expect your partner to love you

If you don't love yourself?

Consider this:

If you don't love yourself, you'll think you're

unlovable and therefore unworthy of love.

And if you feel unworthy of love, it will be difficult for you to establish a solid, committed relationship.

Everybody has heard it before. People find it more attractive to be around people who are confident in who they are and what they have to offer. For your husband nothing has changed.

You need to demonstrate to your husband that you are deserving of his love and attention and that you are easy to love.

Recall your teenage years, when you made your first attempts at dating.

At this age, the majority of us feel anxious and unsure about ourselves. We are, after all, still discovering who we are and where we fit in the universe.

While some fortunate individuals are able to establish enduring relationships at that age, the majority of people cannot. Why? Because they aren't capable of loving themselves sufficiently to be able to accomplish it.

We learn to love ourselves as we mature. That is the theory, at least.

But even the most self-assured person out there may find it challenging to love themselves.

We've been raised to believe that liking oneself is conceited and narcissistic, but in reality the reverse is true.

Give your husband a road map to loving you by demonstrating to him how much you value and care for yourself.

So, how do you develop self-love?

It's undoubtedly challenging, but you must remember that the key is what I like to refer to as "radical acceptance of oneself.

Radical self-acceptance entails recognizing that it's OK to be who you are.

It's more about appreciating the entirety of you, whatever and whoever you are, than it is about accepting your shortcomings.

Nobody is perfect. Everyone errs occasionally. Nobody is without regrets. However, a large portion of our time is spent trying to alter.

We frequently think, "I'd go out and socialize more if I could just lose weight." Or you might say, "If only I were better at networking, I'd go for a promotion."

Radical self-acceptance entails being able to appreciate every aspect of oneself, even the parts you'd rather alter or don't like.

When you are able to do that, you stop impeding your own advancement.

You start pursuing goals and desires just because you want to after you stop thinking that you're not good enough.

It entails declaring that rather than waiting for things to change

, "I am who I am, and I am going to enjoy my life to the fullest today." A man can't help but be

3. Drawn to a woman's bravery when she has the guts to love herself.

Set aside time for enjoyable activities with your partner.

It's simple to forget to enjoy yourself as your marriage progresses.

The more your lives are intertwined, the more time you seem to spend doing chores and hanging out in general rather than going on fun dates and experiences.

This is partially an expected result of being married.

Making a solid, enduring friendship involves more than just having fun all the time and swinging from chandeliers. It also involves doing boring things together.

But regrettably, a husband's "boredom" might be a crucial factor in his loss of love.

Keep the following in mind:

Just because you're married doesn't imply that the fun's done

You must take great care to avoid making your relationship entirely about spending less and staying in the budget. There is no either/or situation here.

You know the saying "I love you but I'm not in

love with you" when a relationship ends? Frequently, it just implies "we don't do fun things together anymore."

A connection is woven together by shared enjoyment. It plays a significant role in your bond.

At first, the main focus was on having fun. It can't be anything right now. However, you can be sure that it is still a sizable feature.

How you carry this out Even though it's dull, set aside some enjoyable time.

If it isn't occurring naturally, you must take steps to ensure that it does so.

Perhaps a weekly Sunday movie date, or just a steamy night in every now and then. Whatever you and your hubby find acceptable.

4. Ensure he feels necessary.

I am aware of how times have changed and how popular strong, independent women are right now. Males, however, like to feel needed.

Put it down to men's evolutionary history of being the relationship's defender and provider.

Men naturally want to put you at ease and give you a sense of security.

However, your husband may lose faith in both the relationship and himself if he feels that he isn't actively required in your life.

I understand that you likely have your own life under control, but why not ask your husband to take care of something for you? Just that. Just ask for assistance.

You'll not only offer him something to do—after all, he is your husband and wants to support you—but you'll also see how eager he is to assist you.

Tell your hubby you'll be depending on him. Another way to state it is.

The best part is that this is precisely what he wants.

Why?

He has a deep-seated desire to be a hero every day.

5. Ensure your husband feels appreciated.

Make your husband feel as though he has earned your respect if you want him to rediscover his love for you.

To put it another way, you must help him feel like a hero (not exactly like Thor, though).

I realize how absurd it sounds. Women don't need to be rescued in the modern world. They don't require a "hero" to save them.

And I wholeheartedly concur.

The ironic reality is this, though. Men still require heroic qualities. They seek connections that enable them to feel like one since it is ingrained in their DNA to do so.

Men are clamoring for your awe. For the women in their lives, they want to take responsibility and gain their respect. This has a strong biological foundation in men.

The real kicker?

In the event that this thirst is not quenched, a man won't be content in his marriage.

Relationship psychology actually has a phrase for what I'm referring to here. The hero instinct is what it's known as.

Now, showing him your praise the next time you meet him won't make him feel like a hero. Men dislike being recognized for simply showing up. Believe me.

A man wants you to think that he respects him.

How?

When you know what to do, there is an art to doing this that can be a lot of fun. However, it takes a bit more effort than simply asking him to fix your computer or carry your bulky bags.

Watching this free film on the internet is the ideal way to discover how to make your husband feel like a hero. James Bauer, a relationship expert, talks about easy things you can do right away to turn on your husband's natural male drive.

You'll notice the results right away if you can successfully arouse this inclination.

A man will behave more kindly, pay closer

attention, and put more effort into your marriage if he truly believes that he is your hero.

6. Practice saying "thank you"

We all enjoy being recognized, so it should come as no surprise that we sometimes neglect to express our gratitude to our spouses for the little things they do.

Stop doing that and start saying "thank you" to your husband for everything he does for you.

These two words will certainly strengthen your bond.

You probably don't remember to thank your husband for a lot of the typical things he does for you, like taking you to work or fixing a broken faucet.

So observe what happens when you develop the habit of being appreciative of what your husband does.

The significance of making your husband feel needed was discussed above. The situation is exactly the same here.

He'll feel more valuable if you learn to praise him and appreciate what he does, and that will undoubtedly improve his mood in your marriage.

7. Give him a big hug and a hello whenever you see him.

Ignore what most people advice. Little things do matter.

We all say hello and goodbye on a daily basis, and for the most part, we fall into the habit of being very bland and monotonous about it.

However, if you offer your husband a loving embrace and kiss each time you see him after work, or even when you bid him farewell in the morning, he'll feel pretty darn good about himself.

He may easily develop this habit, and it will make him feel better every time he returns home from work.

Spend some time telling your husband how much you'll miss him when he's gone and how eager you are to see him again. It will do wonders for your marriage.

Watch Brad Browning's little video here for additional straightforward and sincere advice on how to get your husband back.

8. Test out the 10-minute rule.

The 10-minute rule may be familiar to you.

I guess your next question is, "What the hell is this 10-minute rule?"

Naturally, in order to participate in this activity, you'll need to prepare some questions beforehand.

Here are a few concepts:

- What do you want to be known for above all else?
- What do you believe to be your best quality?
- What song do you consider to be the greatest of all time?
- What would you change if you could change one thing about the world?

Discussing anything unusual is the point of this conversation. Discuss a topic that interests you!

You might believe that you are aware of each other's opinions on all topics, but I guarantee you'd be mistaken. Everyone has more information to learn.

Heck, you could even talk about the good times you've shared in the past.

That will undoubtedly cause his mind to wander back to all the passionate and enjoyable times you've shared.

9. Want suggestions tailored to your circumstance?

While the major strategies for getting your husband to love you again are covered in this article, it can be beneficial to discuss your issue with a relationship coach.

When you work with a certified relationship coach, you can get advice that is suited to your life and your experiences.

On the website Relationship Hero, highly qualified relationship counselors offer assistance to those going through complex and challenging romantic situations, such as reigniting a marriage's passion. They are a very well-liked resource for anyone dealing with difficulties of this nature.

How am I aware?

So, a few months ago, when my own relationship was having a hard time, I contacted Relationship Hero. They provided me with a new perspective on the dynamics of my relationship and how to get it back on track after I had been so mired in my own thoughts.

I was amazed by my coach's kindness, sensitivity, and genuine helpfulness.

You can speak with a certified relationship coach in just a few minutes to obtain guidance tailored to your requirements.

10.　　**Stand by your boyfriend and offer moral support.**

Being a man is more difficult than you may imagine.

They must have the motivation to take on the role of provider in the relationship and serve as the family's rock during trying times.

Most men learn early on that they must succeed in whatever they do and should never show signs of weakness.

And boy, is there a lot of competition!

This explains why some guys can become agitated and angry.

Additionally, it explains why they require their wife's unwavering support from a distance.

Encourage him if he has goals and objectives of his own. Be his staunchest ally.

Imagine yourself up against the world alone, and you'll be supporting him to ensure your mutual success.

In fact, this is a problem that a lot of couples face, especially in toxic relationships.

They often criticize one another without recognizing it. This typically occurs in relationships where there is some element of competition and an ongoing striving to outdo one another.

But you know where that ends up, right? As you may guess, resentment and bitterness are quite bad for any relationship.

Be not a part of such unions.

Relationships that are unconditionally supportive of one another are far healthier and more satisfying. Both of you have a lot more room to develop.

11.   Do not attempt to alter him.

There will always be things about being with your partner constantly that bother you, no matter who you are.

This does not imply that you ought to try to make him less bothersome in any way.

People find it extremely difficult to change, and when someone puts constant pressure on them to, they are even less inclined to do so.

Men who are with women who are continually giving them advice on how to do things better have a tendency to become distant from them.

In fact, this is often what makes a man stop being interested in a woman.

So what's my advice?

Be mindful of your language when speaking to

your husband. If you keep telling him, "You should," he might stop being interested in you, so you might want to back off.

Don't get me wrong, though:

I'm not advising you to keep quiet about something he's doing that is significantly impairing your quality of life. Obviously, you should speak up if it's important and could have a negative impact on your future.

However, if they are minor (i.e., little "annoyances"), attempt to view them from a different perspective.

Accept and enjoy his peculiarities. It will make life much simpler for him, and he won't feel under as much pressure to behave differently around you.